Emily's Mothers

Veronica Aaronson

For one human being to love another;
that is perhaps the most difficult of all our tasks.
Rainer Maria Rilke

Emily's Mothers

© Veronica Aaronson

First Edition 2020

Veronica Aaronson has asserted their authorship and given their permission to Dempsey & Windle for these poems to be published here.

Published by Dempsey & Windle
15 Rosetrees
Guildford
Surrey
GU1 2HS
UK
01483 571164
dempseyandwindle.com

British Library Cataloguing-in-Publication Data

A catalogue record for this book is available from the British Library

ISBN: 978-1-913329-31-0

Front cover: *On Dartmoor* by Fay Anderson

For
my children Simon, Anna, Tom and Matthew
and my birthmother Freda.

Acknowledgements:

Thanks to the editors of the magazines and anthologies in which these poems originally appeared:

Graham Clifford for awarding 'My Longing To Have Ash Blonde Hair Begins' second place in Waltham Forest Competition 2019

Paul McGrane for nominating 'My Longing To Have Ash Blonde Hair Begins' for the *Forward Prize* and for including it in the *Where I'm From* anthology

Michael Longley for including 'Day Out 'on the short list of the *Rialto* Nature Competition (2018):

Amina Alyal and Edwin Stockdale for including
The Mother I Would Have Liked in : *An Insubstantial Universe –*

Charles and Katerina at *Obsessed With Pipework* for accepting:
'Breaking the Spell'
'The Tea Party '
'I Do. ...Don't I?
'The Teenage Mother'

Thank you to those who commented on earlier versions of these poems: Matthew Aaronson, Kim Bour, Helene Demetriardes and Rebecca Gethin.

Contents

My Longing To Have Ash Blonde Hair Begins

I'm standing.
I'm in front of the fire.
Mother's second pair of eyes stare down
from her portrait above the mantelpiece.

There's no warning fanfare, just
a clearing of Mother's throat:
We have something to tell you.
We're not your real parents

      Your   mother

seventeen
                not   married

couldn't   keep   you

The words float
like   fluff   blown
from   a   dandelion   head
             in stilled air.

As the seeds settle,
I feel no grief or gratitude, only relief.
Now I understand why
the three of us are only tacked together with cotton,
not stitched in silk thread.

I ask the colour of my real mother's hair.

Sitting Targets

Mother stores her resentments as if they're food
to help her survive harsh winters.
Her loaded gun's always ready. She watches
from her hide till she spots a weakness,
then aims for the forehead,
sometimes the heart.

Daddy rarely speaks, but when he does
he strips his words to their core
– calls me *Emi* and Mother *Sylv*.
He knows speech can attract attention,
place you in the firing line.

I keep my head tucked in,
stick to the unheated, unlit corners
to reduce my chance of being
stamped on   now
now or
now.

Family Likeness

I watch Daddy shaving

When he goes down to breakfast

     I drag a stool to the basin

stretch my fingers towards

                    a blade

he's not yet thrown in the bin

I pinch my cheek   watch the edge sink in

It stings

     gloop dribbles   towards my chin

I tear a corner of toilet paper

                press hard till the blood soaks in

take away my hand

     the paper sticks just like Daddy's

I grin.

Family Unlikeness

Mother has ebony curls.
My hair is blonde and straight.

Mother's squat.
I'm lanky.

Mother looks tanned.
My skin's pale.

Mother has bedroom eyes.
Mine are full-mooned.

Mother's nose is straight.
Mine's curved.

And still they say,
She's so obviously your daughter.

I want to scream:
Don't be ridiculous!

*Anyone can see she's nothing
to do with me!*

I cage my tongue behind
the barb of my teeth

and keep swallowing.

Permanent Wave

Mother moans as if she's in pain,
*You'll never find a man with
your straight-as-a-broomstick hair.*

She winds my hair around curlers
made from hedgehog hide, presses
a sodden sponge against my skull.
Her magic potion stings my eyes.

There's no beauty without pain.

Her spell takes time to work. She rolls
a fag, flicks the ash in the sink,
puffs on it till it's a butt.

I'm still, silently cursing her
and every mirror in the house.

A cascade of water blocks my nose.
Can't breathe, I splutter.

*Don't make such a fuss!
There's no beauty without pain.
No beauty without pain.*

The Empty Shell

As if they're gelignite,
Daddy's campaign medals are wrapped
in a blanket on the top shelf of his wardrobe.
Now he's back on civvy street he distracts himself
from *all that.*

Mornings he lights the fire,
polishes shoes, boils eggs, eats his, then disguises
his empty shell upside-down in my egg cup.
I feign surprise at the hollow crack.

My soldiers relax, redundant on the side of my plate.
He laughs as if he's just outwitted the enemy,
then louder and louder, till we're guffawing
like squaddies letting off steam on a Friday night.
His face distorts. He clutches his sides.

Mother has grown tired of this game,
shouts like a Sergeant Major: *Stop this racket!*
You two are getting on my nerves!

The Mother I Would Have Liked

Mrs. Craig takes me to the library, points me towards
Captain Ahab, D'Artagnan, Allan Quatermain.

She lends me her clothbound edition of *Mill on the Floss*.
I bond with Maggie Tulliver.

Maggie knows what it's like to have a mother
who can only imagine her daughter as a wife.

Mother perms my hair too tight,
I look ridiculous! I spit. She doesn't care what I say.

Like Maggie, I hack at my hair. Mother spits,
You look ridiculous! I don't care what she says.

I rush to Mrs. Craig's.
She listens, strokes what remains of my hair.

Day Out

Most of all I remember Mother passing me a hanky
because of the stench in the elephant house,
eating my ice cream quickly,
while the rain hit the ground with force, and
the lone polar bear pacing like clockwork
on the edge of his enclosure, left to right,
lifting his front paws, pivoting, right to left,
not stopping for a moment,
padding half-heartedly,
as if he'd given up all hope.

As if he'd given up all hope,
padding half-heartedly,
not stopping for a moment,
lifting his front paws, pivoting, right to left
on the edge of his enclosure, left to right –
the lone polar bear pacing like clockwork
while the rain hit the ground with force. And
eating my ice cream quickly
because of the stench in the elephant house.
Most of all I remember Mother passing me a hanky.

Breaking the Spell

There's a frog that insists on being part of my life,
tattooed in red on his back are the words:
Illegitimate and *Bastard*.

I show him to would-be friends before he jumps out,
and frightens them away.

When I introduce him to Sue, she doesn't see
what I and others see.

She's heard about the golden ball, knows my frog's
a prince waiting to be kissed.

Oh, lucky you! she says, *I've always wanted to be
a love child!*

Clothed in Thunderclouds

This morning Mother's out of cigarettes,
has spilt the milk and blames Daddy.

What have you ever done other than make my life more
*   difficult!*
Even Emily's more use than you!
I shrink trying to dull my shine.

When Daddy's low enough, she stands
over him, one foot on his back,
rifle slung over her shoulder,
congratulates herself.

She'd mount his head on a plaque if she could,
instead she chalks up her hits
on an imagined blackboard, each strike
the shape of a crucifix.

Missing

Grandmother lost her husband, whether through
natural causes, war or carelessness no one lets on.
If his name's mentioned, her lips clamp so tight
they buckle and her cheeks puff out, like an octopus
about to spurt ink, before she dives off into
a different room.

She has survived the craters of misfortune.
has learnt how to suck grit, roll it on the roof
of her mouth until it hardens to mother-of-pearl.
She spits out each gem, threads it on string, wears
them like campaign medals.

The Kitbag

It's gone half past two.
Mother's out.
Daddy's kitbag squats on the table.

He rifles through the family album,
slips out photos, layers them between
pages of a Dennis Wheatley book,
puts the book in the kitbag.

He's as unruffled as last night's bed sheets,
as sure of himself as
a man who's downed a bottle of whisky.

His footsteps echo as if he's marching on stone,
or perhaps the space in my skull has lost its lining.

You'll be alright. You're old enough now.
He kisses me on the cheek,
as though he's just popping out.

The walls shiver.
My legs feel like they might snap.
Daddy swings the kitbag over his shoulder,
then escapes
through the front door.

Gossip

Imagine a woman who can make meringues
that are gooey in the middle.

Imagine a woman who can knit, crochet and
use a sewing machine.

Imagine a woman who can speak German,
Russian and French fluently.

Imagine a woman who can play the piano,
guitar and mouth organ.

Imagine a woman who can dance the Tango,
the Cha-cha-cha and the Fandango.

Imagine a woman who regularly threatens
to leave her husband.

Imagine that woman's surprise when her husband
walks out on her.

My Feet in God's Boots

I'm between

wakefulness and   sleep.

A plastic bottle rattles

I imagine Mother swallowing pills.

When I wake

the air's as still as a dodo's breath

I read her note

the pendulum swings

her wishes   my wishes   her wishes

should I? shouldn't I? should I?

I pick up the receiver.

The dial

crawls

9   9   9.

The Tea Party

The hospital's a warren. Signs to the Clifton Ward
say *This way*, change their mind to *That way*.

Mother's white jacket is on back to front,
her arms hidden behind her back.
She rallies the ward's inmates.
Here she comes! Look at her. Couldn't leave well alone!

Her troops are as flimsy as playing cards.
One smiles like a toothless Cheshire cat and disappears
under the bedclothes. Another lies as quiet as a dormouse
in a perfectly made up bed, staring at the ceiling.
Another paces, muttering.

Mother's needle keeps going,
So selfish, only ever thinks of herself!

I send regards from Mrs. Kerin.
Let her know the cat's turned up
and I've paid the milkman.

The clock's tock-tick only quickens
when a round ball of a woman
arrives with the tea trolley.
Afternoon. And how are we today?
You're looking better.
She offers to hold the cup to Mother's zipped lips.

How do you THINK I feel, stupid woman?!

I drink my tea.
I ask about a vase for the roses.
I make a display of looking at my watch,
lie about bus times, place my lips on her forehead
and walk away to the sound of
Off with their heads!

On Release

I wash Mother, dress Mother, comb Mother's hair,
take Mother to the toilet, peel potatoes, shell peas,
chop cabbage, feed Mother, wash up, sweep the lino,
collect clothes from the floor, wash them, peg them
on the line.

I take in

        air

when I can.

       A large house spider runs towards Mother.
       She stumbles back, hand over mouth.
       I stamp on it.
       CRUNCH!
       A squeal escapes my lips, gives voice to the one
       who's tied into the strait jacket.

Why Can't I Know who my Birthmother Is?

Does she live in a house made of candy,
or one twirling on chicken legs?

Was I taken from her because she'd ordered
 a huntsman to cut out my heart?

Did she lead me deep into a forest and leave me there?
Does she eat children? Is she really a wolf?

Or is she scrubbing floors, blackening grates
for a wicked step-mother,

being held prisoner in a tower, forced
to spin gold?

Maybe she risked her life smuggling me
to safety?

Or did I fall from her womb while she danced on,
on and on in her red shoes?

In the Wrong Nest

I don't fit in this basket balanced on reeds.
I shiver in these wet lands. I dream of a home
where warm winds whistle through tall grasses,
where others sing the same two clear notes.

On Leaving Home at Sixteen

I carry a change of clothes,
an apple and a five-pound note.

In my lungs I carry the taste
of new air and fresh possibilities.

I carry a lesson
from all the females in my life:

Don't trust men, they don't hang around.
Close to my heart I carry Rumi's Love Poems.

I know I can trust him
not to up sticks and leave.

Flashback (i)

First day of school.
My own coat peg.

A sandpit.   A slide
and

a Wendy house.
        A Wendy house!

I can't wait to play.

But when the mothers are asked to leave,
several children start crying.

I hang back,
trying to work out what I'm missing

– what could be so upsetting
in this Aladdin's cave.

On Longing

An aye-aye lives under my skin,
tells me we met long ago in a rainforest.

Now and then she taps the bark of my body,
pokes my flesh with her long fingers.

I've tried nourishing her — singing lyrics by Cohen,
reciting Plath poems, playing the Blues.

I've tried ignoring her,
but nothing stills her for long.

When I give her notice, tell her she's too much,
she looks at me with her large, pleading eyes.

If they don't change my mind, she whispers,
Remember, if I go, you'll lose the only thread to
the source of your yearning.

Taking Family Matters Into My Own Hands

I hunt for pictures that feed me, cut them out from
the National Geographic and other magazines —

stone circles on Dartmoor, an ancient oak at Kew,
a polar bear, a murmuration of starlings, add

portraits I admire of: Carl Jung, Ernest Shackleton,
Martin Luther King, Sitting Bull, Freda Kahlo,
Mahatma Gandhi, then

postcards of Van Gogh's *Sunflowers*, Nicholson's
Green Goblet and Blue Square, *Monet's Poppies*

and photos of: Henry Moore's *Mother with Child*,
Tony Lattimer's *Pregnant Silence*, Elizabeth Frink's *Riace*.

I arrange them on my bedroom wall, glue my photo
near the ceiling.

I'm the fairy on top of my up-side-down family tree.
I link us with indelible ink.

Adoption Papers

It was by private arrangement!

Were they friends?
Did they spend weekends together?
Did they talk about me casually over a pint?

I was nearly two!
Old enough to walk and talk!
How was I passed from one to the other?

Was I picked up by my birthmother, handed to Mother?
Did Mother take me by the hand, pull me away?
Or was I strapped into a pushchair and wheeled away?

Did I turn back, crying *Mummy*?

Trying to Imagine

What must it have been like
when I lost my birthmother?
Was I frightened?
How did I survive?

When I lost my birthmother
my whole landscape must have changed.
How did I survive
when everything I knew vanished?

My whole landscape must have changed,
like a shift from Earth to Mars.
When everything I knew vanished
it must have been difficult to breathe,

like a shift from Earth to Mars.
Did I sob uncontrollably?
It must have been difficult to breathe.
Did I have enough breath to scream?

Did I sob uncontrollably
when I found myself without her?
Did I have enough breath to scream
or did I just wilt?

When I found myself without her
was I frightened
or did I just wilt?
What must it have been like?

The Teenage Mother

A young girl roughly my age joins my Circle Line train.
She's carrying a baby.

We've both snogged long-haired boys behind sheds,
gone a bit further,

but I'm still playing with lipsticks, mascara, rolling over
my waistband, while

she's half-awake, dragging her feet in shoes several sizes
too large.

She's been dealt the Queen of Spades in a game of Black Maria
and can't get shot of it.

If this were a game of Monopoly I'd give her my Get Out
Of Jail Free card. Instead

I imagine us playing Ding Dong Ditch — we wait till dark,
ring the vicar's doorbell, run away,

leave   baby   on the doorstep.

The Match

We're from different countries.
Our paths cross in Amsterdam.

I don't fall in love,
there's no queasiness, rope legs, instead
I melt the way candle wax dissolves, pools
around the wick,
                    overflows,
changes shape
and there's no going back.

Parting was difficult.
I might have wriggled out
of my over-politeness,
told him how I felt,
had Mother's words not echoed,
Men suck you in, then spit you out,
you out, out,   out,   out.

So instead I convinced myself
the striking of the match and
the heat it gave off
were nothing special.

The *O* Word

We spend our first term together.
I'm invited for New Year.

We small-talk with his parents,
nuzzle each other,
run upstairs giggling.

Next morning
his mum serves lumpy porridge.
I devour mine smiling.

Washing the dishes, she mumbles,
At least this one's made me a cup of coffee.

I wonder what the others were like.
The Others.

The Lepidopterist

I'm
    mid-
        flight
            on the stairs,
when his hand clamps my shoulder
while he's talking to someone else.

I'm trapped,
        flap.

When he turns and speaks,
        I chloroform his words
        but
they refuse to still,
    instead flutter
        around in my head.

He sugars his net with jasmine nectar,
syrup distilled from Sufi poetry,
trickery stolen from the gods.

When he squeezes my thorax
between his forefinger and thumb,
pins me to a board,
I don't make a fuss.
I'm his prime specimen.
What could be safer?

If Beds Could Talk

Something's going on.
Usually she sleeps in shabby hand-me-down sheets,
but tonight she's dressed me in virgin linen and lace,
plumped pillows, pulled the duvet into shape
and rearranged the bedside table.

I hear doorbell chimes, chatter, percussion of cutlery,
chinking of glass, voices crescendo, footsteps on the stairs.

His naked body is floorboard-brown, like mine.
His head is topped with wispy curls, like pillow feathers.
She and he are so distracted rolling and rocking on my ribcage,
they don't notice the sliver of moonlight on my headboard.

It's only once they're asleep I notice
her dress-knickers-bra are joined-up-writing,
like a signature across the floor, while
his trousers and shirt have been neatly folded,
his shoes tucked under my frame.

Mother Gives Her Advice Loudly on the Tube

Your boyfriend is a fair bit older, so he might
want to have sex with you soon. Her voice
isn't covered by the rattle of the train.
        It takes centre stage.

Don't worry if the first time is all mess
and no pleasure. It's about building
a relationship, getting to know each other's
likes and dislikes.

I avoid glances in my direction.
Her advice comes way too late, but I smile
graciously. She carries on: *Some men like...*
She projects her voice like an Oscar-winner.

Be inventive, don't let it get stale.
I had a lover who liked me to ...
Once I nearly...
Heads turn, readers look up, others smirk.

I pull the brim of my hat towards my nose,
try to blend in with the seat fabric. Inside
I'm puffing up like a frog, about to explode,
on the brink of letting the audience know

I've no idea who she is and I've been
at it for years, when we arrive at Green Park.
The doors open. I rush out for fresh air.
She   follows   leisurely.

I Do,   Don't I?

I'm wobbling.
My wedding dress is too tight.
It's as restricting as a cocoon.
Or is it the high-heels?

What else could it be?
He's offering me a home.
He says he loves me
and won't leave me.

But he can have a temper.
He threw his cat against the kitchen wall
and he doesn't like my friends.

It's too late to call off the wedding –
guests have bought hats, dresses,
hired suits and travelled miles.

Wings take off in my stomach
as I'm led towards the ring.
I stutter down the aisle.

Later he fumbles to undo
my satin buttons from their loops,
then, only then, I remember:

if a butterfly is helped from its chrysalis,
it struggles to fly. I breathe in, shrink away
from the fabric, away from his fingers.

Pregnant Pause

We dance through the last months —
me: care-free, confident,
baby: coddled in the tight-drum-skin of my belly.
I feed us chunks of Turkish Delight,
giggle when we can't slide through tight gaps.

I imagine fingers winding round mine,
a vest neck soaking up breast milk,
sweetness drenching my nostrils.

The cord's round baby's neck

    each push tightens the noose

        The heart monitor gasps

  then dies.

Silence.

I feel the scissor snip

    baby's corpse being yanked from me

I close my eyes, plunge into the darkness

search every corner

squeeze into every crevice

listening for leftover whispers

trying to find any trace

of my only known blood relation.

A warm weight lands on my stomach

I open my eyes

see his chest rising

and rising.

The Art of Tracing Family Likenesses

Before the birth,
I try to imagine
the shape of my baby's face,
colour of his hair and eyes,
but without family clues it's no use.

I pray that the plains of his cheeks,
incline of his nose,
curve of his eyebrows
will be familiar landscapes.

When he arrives, he's a Monet montage.
Skin: water-lily-white
Eyes: poplar-blue
Hair: haystack-yellow
(just like mine).

He's an impression of what's to come
and because his frame holds
rough sketches of

his ancestors,
(my ancestors),

I want to fast forward to find out what we share, what will
                                        speak our family line,
and I want
the slow reveal,
to study him
day to day
in the changing light,
capture each image,
work out who he is,
who I am.

Different Foregrounds

Sandra enjoys writing letters,
invites me to reminisce —
us making jam with Mother,
fingers stained black from berrying,
trampolining on my parents' bed,
dancing in our garden shed in skirts
made from gingham curtains,
singing while Mother played guitar.

I enjoy reading her letters, remembering
the fun times, but when I try to put ink to paper
shadows overwhelm me —
being woken by Mother's rage, sitting
on the stairs in my nightie, peering
through the bannisters, watching
words, eggs, glass being
hurled at my father, wishing
it would stop.

What the Social Worker Said

Before you see your full birth certificate,
before you trace your birthmother, you need to
prepare yourself for the worst.

She might have been a prostitute.
          You might be the product of rape.
She might be in a mental institution
          or prison.
She might be an alcoholic or drug user.
          She might not want to know you.
She might not have given you a second thought
          She might have emigrated.
She might be dead.

Remember above all else,
Remember above all else:
          She might have kept you a secret.
Her family might know nothing about you.

The Birth Certificate

It lands on the doormat in a slim envelope
that belies the size of what's inside

my heart's ba-booming as if I'm about
to defuse a bomb

I place it on the table face up   continue
spooning soup

I pick up the butter knife slide it
under the seal

pray it doesn't blow up in my face
I pull out the paper

Agnes   seventeen   an office clerk

I allow her name to claim me   feel
the heat of the branding iron

I read her name out loud
Agnes Agnes Agnes

each sound dents the air like
a firecracker.

The Journey

I've seen my birthmother on the tube,
in parks, cafés, through train windows as
they pull out of stations.

She's been the lollypop lady, the librarian,
the actress, the woman sat next to me on
the bus, the singer on Top of the Pops.

She's turned up at school pretending
to be someone else's mum, has passed me
in the street smiling.

She's the one who stops everything
to soothe her baby in the supermarket,
to feed feral cats and stroke stray dogs.

The train's out of sync with my heartbeat
— it slumps between stops as if
it's on a go-slow.

Will I recognise her?

Will she like me?

What if she doesn't?

What if she hates feral cats?

What shall I ask her first?

Is this a gigantic mistake?

She's made of my skin, my eyes, my hair,
my flushed cheeks, moves at my pace,
speaks in my tones.

We both order vegetarian food and herbal teas
make our enquiries formally, politely, like
the strangers we are.

Finding It Difficult to Trust

I can't believe this woman's a mother —
she oozes kindness:
Gosh! You look just like your father.
He was very good-looking.

She feeds me tit-bits, slices of Turkish delight,
pieces snapped off a gingerbread house:
My parents threw me out out.
I gave birth in a Home for Unmarried Mothers.
We stayed with your paternal grandmother.
I tried to find lodgings.
No one would give us a room.
I paid a woman to look after you, visited when I could.

She studies my face, adds:
I became under-nourished, exhausted.
There was a couple who'd lost three babies.
They were desperate.

I swallow her words whole,
regurgitate them when I'm alone.
I need to work out whether
she's grooming me,
fattening me up for the oven, or
casting a spell so I can go to the ball.

Flashback (ii)

Scared I'll be left in the dark,
my four-year old legs chase up
the spiral stairs.

At the top Daddy gushes: *Just look at that view!*
He puts his hands around my middle,
dangles me in front of the battlement.
My coat rides up, my body slips down.

I am sure his hands will let go.
I imagine the sound of rushing air,
the THUD of hitting concrete.

All Dressed Up

Showing Agnes photos, she's drawn to
a professional portrait I've only ever glanced at.

It's of a five-year-old Shirley Temple lookalike.
There's a velvet bow beside her parting.

Her legs have been arranged under the skirt of
a smocked satin dress.

I remember the tightness of those sleeves,
the burn marks they left.

Agnes sees a smiling child seated on a table
in a party dress.

My eyes home in on the crusted scab just above
her left elbow.

The Ashtray

Mother's cigarettes were
carriages of a slow moving train –
they followed one after another,

made lots of smoke and helped her
travel calmly from here to there.
At home,

her favourite ashtray followed
her around the house like
a faithful dog.

I'd watch the lid spin, lower itself
as she pushed the plunger
to hide the butts.

When friends came over, I'd push
the plunger so the exotic aroma
entered our nostrils,

and we heard the hypnotic rhythm.
Mother would shout,
Stop playing with that ashtray!

Clearing out Mother's house,
I find it skulking in a cupboard.
I lift it to my nose and give it one last spin.

It doesn't take me back to childhood,
but to the acrid taste
of our final kiss.

Flashback (iii)

I offer Mother a mud pie,
               wait for her delight.
You're filthy!   Look at that dress!

She pulls me upstairs,
stops
         mid-
               flight:
The neighbours say you don't love me.

I don't understand the words,
         only know
                 something about me's
                     not right.

I look down, tuck my red face
                out of sight.

If Mother Came Back as a Crow

She'd shadow me, back hunched, neck lowered,
readying her claws.

Come spring, before our neighbour shot at
anything black that landed on his land,

I'd load a trap with fresh meat, lure her inside,
risk ripped flesh to keep her alive.

Fixing the Tear

While I'm still scanning crowds
for that ash blonde woman
who looks like me
and Agnes is trying
to reassure herself
that I don't resent her
for giving me up

> a track of bare loam invites us
> through a bluebell carpet
> we inhale scent   tread
> cautiously   negotiate scrub

our paths cross
in and out of each other's lives
as if we're darning
stitch by stitch   until

> we reach a clearing where
> curved ground is covered
> in new shoots
> is an emerald ball
> vibrant
> against sapphire sky and

our weaving becomes solid
invisible to the eye

> from this place it's difficult
> to imagine that anyone
> could have believed
> the Earth was flat.

On Dartmoor

Because Agnes insists only silver birch twigs will do, we leave
the track, stroll onto the open moor, all the time trying to find
landmarks to re-trace our steps.

And because when we turn back, we see the wind has whistled every
hawthorn into crowns of thorns and our landmark rocks look like
every other rock,

we look around to find our bearings, watch the sun's pregnant belly
emerge from behind a cloud and notice
the quality of the silence.

And because we'd been talking about yearning, it isn't the kind of
silence you hear on entering a church, or standing alone on
a mountain top. It has more body.

Somehow all our longing has let loose its sweetness and for a few
moments, we're lost in it together.

The Rush

It's just before leaf fall at Westonbirt Arboretum.
Agnes' mobility scooter stutters on concrete, as if
the battery's running out.

She waits politely, while I negotiate the sodden grass,
read tags, shout back, *Incense Cedar*; *Sea Buckthorn*;
Persian Ironwood Tree,

                                                       but
at the Tulip Tree, as if she's had one cider too many,
she slams her foot down,
races towards me scarring the lawn.

She's leaning into the wind, hair splayed out behind her
sixteen again, she's zooming down a lane
on the back of a Harley Davidson
clinging to her first love.

The Day They Found Agnes' Body

It's 5th August 2012, 1.40pm. Andy Murray's in the Olympic Finals. I'm about to sit down when I see a wall of water speeding down the valley towards me. It lifts plant pots, hurls them against brick, gathers watering cans, deckchairs, water seeps through cracks round the French windows. I gather up Indian rugs, clear books from bottom shelves, move magazines, table, stool, shoes, heave amplifiers upstairs, retreat to the kitchen, pray it doesn't reach the sockets or come under the kitchen door. My car floats across the bridle path into a field. Water starts to ooze up between the floor-boards.

My mobile rings.

On Losing Agnes

Allowing myself to love
and be loved by her,
I'm sweated awake,
dizzied, as if the Earth had
begun spinning in the opposite direction.
My heart and liver wave their red flags
No! You'll get hurt!
My stomach cramps.
My throat forgets how to swallow.
Food is bland.
Her being takes up all the space in my head.
My words are muddled, except for her name,
which balances itself on the

                            tip of my tongue,

ready to spring off.

Now robed in black,
I'm on the same ground,
not sure if I'm dream-ing or nightmare-ing.
I wake flushed,
disbelief staggers around me,
I'm caught in a whirlpool,
screaming *No!*
can't eat.
I'm bent over clutching my stomach.
Her un-being overwhelms me.

Agnes' Gift

Days that were only shot in black and white,
have revealed their colour.

I'm no longer a piece of patchwork tacked with
cotton,

that might be unpicked or come loose of its
own accord.

I've been threaded and knotted onto a sturdy
string, like a pearl.

My longing has been replaced by the richness
of grief for someone known.

Agnes is a wordless lullaby, a reassuring warp
running through the weft of my body.

POSTSCRIPTS

What the Therapist Said About Bonding

Bonds between adoptees and the adopting parents may take time to develop because:

a) bonding begins in the womb,

b) the adopting parents are coming to terms with the fact that they'll never have their own offspring,

c) the adopting parents are grieving for a a baby or babies that miscarried,

d) the relationship feels wrong at an unconscious level,

e) the adoptee is grieving the loss of his/her birthmother,

f) in their grief, adopted children are prone to being either aggressive or withdrawn which makes them hard to reach.

II

What the Therapist Said About Leaving Home

Adoptees often leave home at a young age because:

a) they have learnt to rely on their own resources as a creative adjustment against being abandoned, so becoming independent is an easy step,

b) they've only developed superficial bonds with the adopting parents,

c) one or both of their parents are acting out their disappointments with the adoptee, which makes living at home difficult,

d) they fear they may lose their home so they abandon it, so as not to experience abandonment again,

e) leaving home is an unconscious communication from adoptee to parents to let them know how it feels to be abandoned.

III

What the Therapist Said About Forming Relationships

Adoptees, because of an unconscious fear of abandonment, tend to:

a) become people pleasers,

b) put themselves out to avoid conflict,

c) form bonds with others who fear abandonment,

d) mistake over-attentive and controlling behaviour as a sign of affection.